The Inheritance of Grief

The Inheritance of Grief

Poetry & Prose by
Nishi Patel

Copyright © 2022 Nishi Patel
Cover Illustrations and Design by Islam Farid
Interior Illustrations and Design by Nishi Patel

All rights reserved. No part of this book may be used or reproduced in any manner whatsoever without written permission from the author except in the case of brief quotations embodied in critical articles and reviews.

First Edition 2022

ISBN: 979-8-9862294-0-9 (paperback)
979-8-9862294-1-6 (ebook)

Printed in United States of America

CONTENT WARNING:

grief is not linear

take care of potential triggers
such as anger, depression, anxiety, cancer, PTSD
from being a caregiver, and death of a loved one

dad,

*you are so much more
alive to me
even after you've gone*

CONTENTS

Sealed Letters – 1

THE LOSS

Unmaking – 4
Threshold – 5
Trapping – 6
Blame – 8
Fresh Anger – 12
Falling Hope – 13
Hope – 14
Betrayal – 15
The Dam – 16
We – 19
The Aftermath – 20
Cancer – 21
Brain on Cancer – 22
Changing – 23
Three Things – 24
Dark Clouds – 25
Wrong Timing – 26
2015 – 28
Layered Cake – 29
Tumbling – 30
Unsheltered – 31
Lost – 32
My Father's Daughter – 33

The Love You Left Behind – 34
The Case of Wildflowers – 35
My Father – 36
No Regrets – 38

THE COPING

Time Off – 42
Coping – 43
Getting Through – 44
Numbing Time – 45
The Calm – 46
When Expectations Bite Back – 47
A Puzzle – 48
Compassion – 49
Dissociation – 50
Abandonment – 51
Validation – 52
Invalidation – 53
Shadow – 54
Overcast – 55
Exhaustedly – 56
Boundaries – 57
Painfully – 59
First Aid – 60
Blood – 61
All of It – 62
Buried Alive – 63

Explode – 65
Death Anniversary – 68
India Ink – 69
Moments of Relief – 70
Imprisoned – 71
Ice Skating – 72
Text Me – 73
My Response – 74
Me – 75
Competition – 76
Deep Burn – 77
The Ferocious and Gentle Maha Kali – 80
Heartfull-Less – 82
Busy Surviving – 83
Unfertile Grounds – 85

THE HEALING

Plowing – 90
The Desert – 91
Hold – 92
Hoarding – 93
Fooling – 94
Soul Mine – 95
Key – 96
The Darkness to Light – 97
Permission – 98
The Force – 99

Finding Community – 100
Deceit – 101
Old Self – 102
Letting Go – 103
Separating – 105
Realization – 106
Altered State – 107
A River of Grief – 109
Hard Trust – 110
The Choice I Made – 111
Blooming – 112
Balanced Space – 113
Detour – 114
Anchoring – 115
Constellations – 116
Thawing – 117
Little Rememberings – 118
Indian Daughter – 119
Unconditionally – 120
The Book of Forgiveness – 121
Hospice – 123
Acceptance – 126
Declutter – 127
Identity – 128
Finding My Own – 130
The Compass – 131
The Lingering of Grief – 132
Room for Joy – 133

Obligations – 134
Clear Intentions – 135
Quarantine – 136
Consistently Healing – 137
Moving Through – 138
Lifeline – 139
Memory in the Wind – 140
Lighthouse – 141
Fresh Paint – 142
The Inheritance of Grief – 143
All Things in My Realm – 144
Life – 145
Birthright – 146
Writing –147
Reading –148
Acknowledgments – 155

SEALED LETTERS

the conversations
that are so hard
I sit and imagine
how they would go
the river of words
every molecule of emotions

but nothing
not even a drop escapes my mouth
contained
wondering when it's time
waiting
for it to be safe
to pour
my heart to you

the screams under my skin
sealed
I give to you
in these letters

drink

       (please don't pour them down the drain)

THE LOSS

UNMAKING

it keeps coming
the darkness inside the dark
the grave of my grief
a mouth of a new world
I was not given a map
nor told how it would
unmake me

THRESHOLD

and just like that
[the rhythm of] his raspy breath
now nothing but   an echo
the untamed beast
ate every last   piece of him

and just like that
everyone is passing
through the opened door

I could not even release a prayer

I am nothing but a long breath
holding onto   yesterday
I am nothing but a hunger
searching for   distractions

his life now at rest but
awakens the fury in me

TRAPPING

I'm no longer trapped
in taking care of my dad
but now
I'm trapped in
my own grief

time felt like a force against my will
monstrous and unpredictable

BLAME

we should have kept his teeth

we should have gotten an appointment sooner

he should have stopped chewing tobacco sooner

he shouldn't have started in the first place

it was all I could do
to escape the swarming condolences
to keep from tearing open in front of the guests
their footwear by the door
piled upon mine
I settled for my brother's sandals

pushing through the hinged glass
my heart quietly roared

a ticking bomb
trying to remain calm

I secretly wished they would all leave
just going for a walk
surely they'd understand the need
even if it's 10:30 o'clock dark

as soon as the street lined with cars
faded behind me
the backs of rubber began
to slapped against my heels
wished I had on tennis shoes

to run away faster
I swear I could

heart, enraged finally getting to bleed
feet shattering the ground below
mind striking like thunderbolt

why oh why oh why

heart, enraged
gush of red pooled the sky
emotions scattering like stars of stones

the rupture of my viscous wound

I could stay here for eternity
there's nothing else left to do

my head screams
stop!
it's enough now

my head screams
keep going!
do not give up
as if I am *still* fighting for his life

the shrieking echo of his (last) breath
screaming
       in my head

DON'T stop
CAN'T stop
how I have repeated
these words into my being

this is all a dream
with tears on fire
please, I beg You

is it not?

FRESH ANGER

my tears were hardly seen
because anger
caught them first
clenched in my fist
just so I could
have something
to hold

that was before
anger caught hold of me
the end of his life
was the beginning of my death

like being boiled by the sun
as I followed his name into a black hole

FALLING HOPE

it was going to be worth it
removing all of his teeth
to protect from the radiation
eating through a feeding tube
running into his stomach

he was going to have dental implants

he was going to
live
a f t e r
this fight was over

the fight was over
when his life
was taken over

hope overthrown
crowning the cancer

HOPE

that's the thing
with hope and cancer
-constantly telling yourself
there is only one more
thing to do
before it gets better

the hardest part was knowing when
hope was becoming too strong of a gravity
automatic and blinding
as if tethered to the sun

sometimes I wonder if
surrendering would have
been the bravest thing

buying more time worth remembering
rather than always being at war with fate

BETRAYAL

it was supposed to be curable
we did everything we were supposed to do
he was supposed to get better

but he didn't

THE DAM

it was a stark realization

I'm all into the abyss

I shouldn't wallow in my waters
when surely the spouse
of the deceased
is the most grieved
I'm only the daughter

back into the only lighted house
I looked
where is she?

I must now be her pillar

it was she who found me
my mother
soothing my burn
with her words
she's always been
able to see the bigger
picture

I hug myself even tighter

despite my bloodshot eyes
arms of my brother
wrapped around me

his heart seeing mine

> *I do not know how to*
> *carry this softness*

I'm...

swallowing
my own
grief   gasping
       for
       air   as the pain
                scrapes
                down my throat

tears hiccuped like fizzy bubbles
the erratic ripples of air

my glossy glare
locked on my father's limp hands

one by one I picked
up the broken stones
of the dam
reining in
the livid liquid
into the cavity
in my skin

> *back into my heart*

I realized later that
I settled for implosion

but that was okay

as long as I didn't crack

today

WE

we
because we
depended on each other

me leading a way for victory
while he fought in the battlefield
of his body

he put his life in my hands
and
I needed him to stay alive

THE AFTERMATH

I look at myself and see nothing but ruins
my name is no longer a place to call home

CANCER

cancer is
going about your day living in
invisible lightning and stalling thunder
while you wait
for the irreversible damage

cancer is
a trespasser
vandalizing organ to organ

cancer is
a game of catch me if you can

cancer is
a war fighting against
the soul's residence in the body

cancer is
correction fluid on the diary
of memory

cancer is
a birthright hijacked

BRAIN ON CANCER

he fought
    without rest

until his mind
    could no longer
        tell him
            to fight

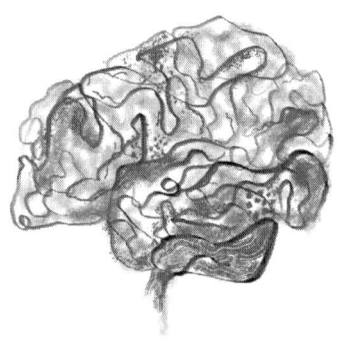

CHANGING

our way of life
gripped
by our mere obsessions

it begs to be changed
when we can no longer bear the weight
of its consequences

do not wait until it's too late
if you are lucky to see another day
maybe that is enough to make
you do one thing
different

THREE THINGS

(you should know)

the only thing that is constant is change
the only thing that is certain is death
the only thing that is yours is today

DARK CLOUDS

I am the sun cloaked behind eyes of grief
the eyes that deny it release

WRONG TIMING

what did you expect?
that I'd grieve later?
cry later?
for you?

by the time you offered your arms to me
I was already hardening

you weren't there
so you don't know

2015

the year was somber
I've become morose

LAYERED CAKE

death is the occasion
in which grief arrives
like a tidal wave
inviting other griefs
from their hiding place

TUMBLING

I have been
running full speed
my life's marathon
of goals
changing professions
with each season of life
where days were short

this whirlwind
tumbled out of its balance
like a spinning top
coming out of its axis
as my earth disappeared
when his soul departed

there's no more gravity
my heart rate still high
how the days now seems like years

UNSHELTERED

for my protection
you've planted a fortress
for my growth
you've manipulated the soil

all that you have built
burned with your
cremation

LOST

not anchored in your guidance
I've been uprooted

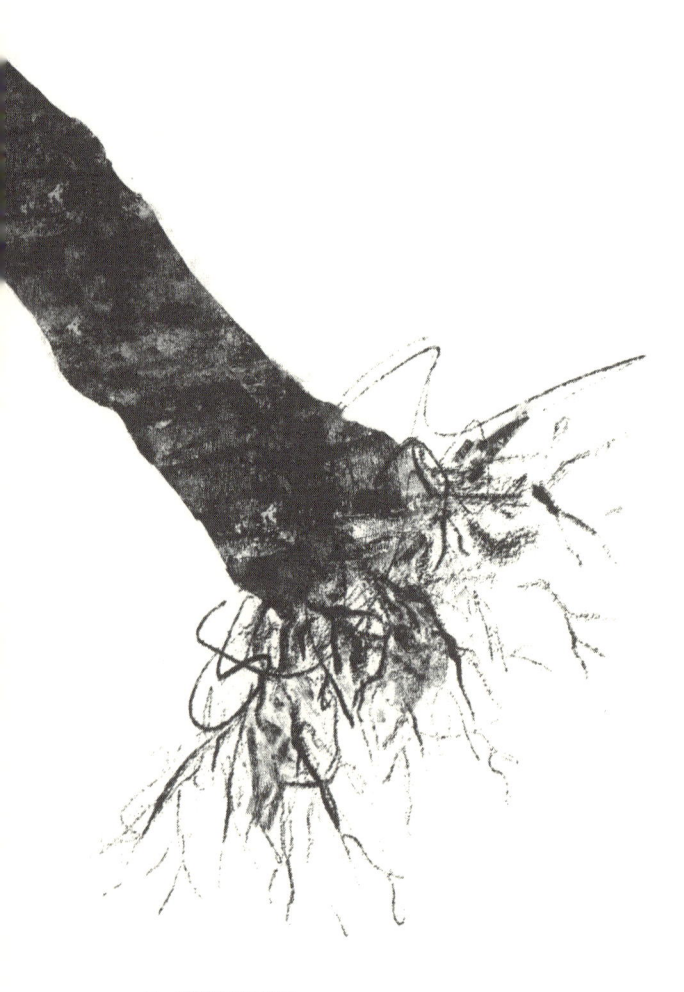

MY FATHER'S DAUGHTER

it wasn't perfect
it was family above all else
it was duty & responsibilities

despite resentments
despite what I wanted
despite hurtful disappointments

I guarded our relationship
I saw vulnerability behind his protectiveness
I hated him and I loved him

I was my father's daughter

THE LOVE YOU LEFT BEHIND

I feel the weight
of your love
even more
after you're gone

your voice comes to me
so clearly I can
feel it and
hear it
resonating in the air
of the room
I wake up in
after the dream

THE CASE OF WILDFLOWERS

you died and now
you're nowhere and everywhere

you're popping up like wildflowers
you're wild and free
as you went away closer

MY FATHER

he traveled across seas to seek
a better life in the land of the free
a life not as a farmer in the cotton field
not bringing his newly-wed wife
but as promised went back for her
that is, after living on 25 dollars
a month as his expenses, ensuring there would be more
in his pocket for a roof over their heads

he went from dollars and a wife
to a family and a business to call his own

he was a man with courage burdened with
worried shoulders, that is how he grew
something from just a little more than nothing
why he offered help to family friends
who also longed for a new beginning

he had a watchful eye
and wise were his words
he was respected and honest
sometimes with truth that hurt

he had a calloused heart, it is how they raised you back home
I always knew that the disjunction
between his genuine caring
and his failed efforts at loving

were both from a pure heart / he fought with us, his
children, as he worried about our future / then silently
ached between remorse and a grudge

I wonder when his worries mulled into bitter love
and when numbing with tobacco
became an addiction

in the final days when he
still had a bit of
coherence left in his head
he said to me
Nishi, I goofed.
I said, no dad
you did the best you could
you did good.

NO REGRETS

I wouldn't have done it any other way
putting myself last
to have your back
all the way until the end

THE COPING

TIME OFF

everybody keeps saying
that it takes time
what are they trying to say?
that I can't heal from this?

they are surprised to hear that I am
taking a break from work

are they saying that I
should keep on moving so
that I don't break down?

maybe they don't realize that
the time it takes to rise out of bed
and hide pain with a smile
is work

COPING

you ask how
am I doing
I tell you what
I've been up to

that's the most I can give you
right now as I am asking
myself the same question

I have not thought
about me in years

(how could I even explain it to you)

GETTING THROUGH

all I know is that
I feel horrible on the inside yet
when I wake up
practice yoga
and drink my coffee
I usually feel okay
enough to bluff my way
through the day's trials
holding onto the repetitive notes
of daily rhythm that keep me afloat
while my head drowns in denial

NUMBING TIME

so this is what it feels like
to sit with time
like a bird sitting on a wire
I could sit here forever
drinking in the stillness
I've been deprived of for so long
a stillness that comes from
completely shutting off my brain
for my mind to go numb
to the chill after the sun grieves
feeling the gloomy peace
of the settling leaves
that leaves me with time
to just sit with me

THE CALM

this is an eerie feeling
this calmness so foreign

is it the slow ripples at the end
of a roaring rapid

or

is it the beginning
of a crashing
waterfall

WHEN EXPECTATIONS BITE BACK

I never called on the ones
who said to let them know
if I needed anything
so they did nothing
and I got nothing
from the ones who I wanted
support from the most

A PUZZLE

maybe I can push my way in
maybe I can skim off parts of me

I am searching for a community
but don't seem to fit anywhere
and nothing seems to fit me

COMPASSION

I shut down my emotions
    but open up to yours
I stop my crying
    but tell you to keep crying
I tell you that it's okay
    to go through
        what you're going through

why do I keep telling myself
it isn't okay for me
to be human too?

DISSOCIATION

his death sent me worlds away
I can no longer remember how it feels
to come home to myself

ABANDONMENT

in truth
it's like I have
disowned my own heart

and now I want it back
but I've forgotten how
compassion feels

VALIDATION

I remove myself from
the beast of my grieving body
to step into your moments
to be with you in your grief
to dance with you in your joy
to validate your heart
I'm sorry that it's inconvenient
for you to step into mine

INVALIDATION

my grief gets invalidated
every time I have no choice
but to be okay
and when you ignore me
so that you can be okay

SHADOW

my sorrow lives in shadows
where darkness collects my tears
a place I can count on
unlike out in the open
where people hear them
and carry on

OVERCAST

I've forgotten how to smile
because my smile disappeared
because I stopped smiling
because I was afraid
someone would steal my smile

EXHAUSTEDLY

I shove my grief and pain away
and power through
the appearance
of being collected
while my heart is
exhausted by humanity

BOUNDARIES

life is an overdose
on my nerves
so I give my grieving
body
the space and boundaries
it needs to be nurtured

it's unfair to want so much from you
and resist you just as much

PAINFULLY

I don't need you to make me feel better
I need you to sit with me
and let me feel the pain

FIRST AID

I have to keep my heart
on ice
so that it does not get
burned by grief

BLOOD

it's cruel I know
to want blood on your
hands just so you'd know
how it feels to take the
bullet of anger and remorse
that no words can faithfully convey
how heavily my
wounds are bleeding

until then
your sympathies are meaningless

ALL OF IT

you want into
my mind
my heart?

think twice
because it's all or nothing
I'll give it all to you
until you feel the same pain
that I do

BURIED ALIVE

I continue to burn
myself from the pain

feelings get pruned
emotions cut back
into the roots of my
heart thickly with
screams that are
whispers
to everyone else

*are you going to just
let me slip away?*

EXPLODE

I know about
living life with
a painted smile
on my face
doing what's expected
a mother, a wife, a daughter
no one would ever know

sometimes
my eyes will unfreeze
    to leak a tear
my mouth will unleash
    the faintest plea
       of need

and if someone there
    could see through
    my shield
maybe
    just maybe
my heart
would spill a little

and maybe
if I felt safe
    after testing you'd stay
my mind
would finally relinquish

    that grip
        on my heart
gushing open
   the liquid heat
     of fire and ice

the anger the pain the grief and hurt
the knots exploding into molten lava

the magnitude of emotions
that lie dormant
s t i l l

timing has it
   right there in
the shopping aisle
the hot shower
the drive home
where there is no one
no one to see
t h r o u g h
my cracked window
and notice
this darkness in my chest
that pumps through my veins

numbness pressing against a racing heart
I'm breathing but there's
n o   a i r
it hurts so bad
the heaviness
pulls me further

into the deepest blue
of chaotic silence

and because I don't know what to say
or how to reach out
or maybe it's because
I'm afraid
that if I start crying
I won't be able to stop

that's me trying to function
on the outside
as I swallow it all
my heart
d r o w n i n g
a thousand times over
and no one would ever know

DEATH ANNIVERSARY

I just want to
　run,
　　run,
　　run
and not stop

INDIA INK

I loosen my bra straps but that doesn't fix it
I strip all over again looking for the culprit
to find it's not the clothes I'm wearing but
the dark blob clenching my insides

a nameless thing oozing out from my center
a burden wrapping around my spine
like tentacles with an unceasing grip

this dis-ease transparent to doctors
but it feels so thick and all-
absorbing
as india ink to me

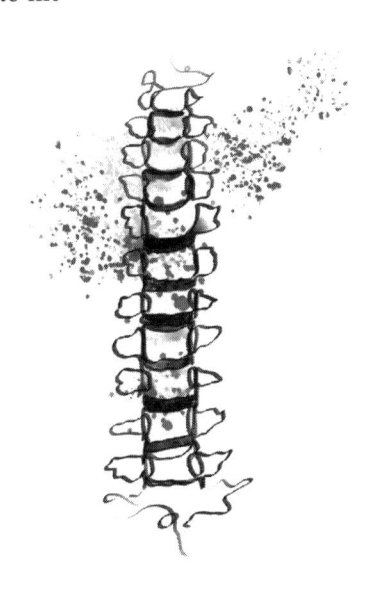

MOMENTS OF RELIEF

I can't get enough of the fresh clean air
that I taste in my chest when I jog
it's a yo-yo of moments
where the darkness inside me
lags behind when neither feet
are touching the ground
I wish I could keep on running forever
because stopping would mean
that the dark blob catches up to my soul
saying I'm still here

IMPRISONED

all that I've endured
churns underneath my skin
slowly turning into stone

my heart
begging for release
my mind
won't let it

I think
I've completely forgotten
how to feel

ICE SKATING

on the ice I can escape
gliding effortlessly to the rush of fresh cool air
that allows my mind to smile

I'm off the ground of reality
and under a spell of peace
even if it's only for a short time
it's been a long time since
I've had this kind of space

TEXT ME

keep texting me without expecting a response
because I have nothing to say but still
need someone to keep me from feeling lonely
so that I am not alone in my sorrow

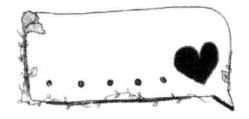

MY RESPONSE

know that I will respond
not with words typing back to you
but within the depths of my inner being
my cells having
something
to hold onto
reminding me that I still exist
even if I'm barely surviving
and reminding me to thank you
when I do come up for air

you will be the first person that I text

ME

courage came
to gather up my deep emotions
and shape them into words

you smashed them down
when you said
<u>me too</u>

(it's just me not you too)

COMPETITION

whose story is this?

I'm tired of playing this game
of who has it worst

DEEP BURN

I can already
feel it
feasting
on my flesh, organs, cells

his physical pain
incarnating within me

I keep his heart beating with
this broken record of his
suffering
    alive in my mind
          my heart
          my veins

my hunger
   to swallow
      my goodbye
         instead of
saying them

how much longer
can I endure
the poison
   of my prisoned heart
guilty and not guilty
please I beg myself
   unbind the chains to my father's death

clouds in my head
hold no more promises
of clarity
rage from the burn
turn thoughts into ashes

salty monsoon meets the
eyes -
waterless on the other side
choking on thunder
of voiceless words

an explosion on the horizon
every single cell of my body
erupting with emotions
all in vain
for my skin is a soundproof membrane

and although
I feel e v e r y t h i n g
my body is numb
unmovable against the deafening
storm within me

high tides of last cries
can anyone hear me?

d
  o
    w
      n   I go into the dark

caved by the ache
there's no end
it's burning my veins

who would dive so deep
into the trenches of my pain
to pull me out

or

have I just given myself the death sentence?

THE FEROCIOUS AND GENTLE MAHA KALI

it feels like some superpower
how else can this body hold
everything it swallows
almost demon-like
befriending it is
anger devouring itself
and here I am
at the point of a sword
crescent-shaped in
my bloody hands
fragments of my
mirrored self
like earth's
dirt

how mortality looks me in the eye
unveiling who I am in all my terrors
enter, oh Dark One - strong and boundless
unapologetic force of nature
not wild but like wilderness

the essence of grief
relentlessly fighting to
simply exist
for holding is stagnant
a true destruction (of my own flesh)

I no longer want to disappear

in the name of self-suffering
You must be a presence of healing I taste
my palms trembling at the tenderness
of this invincible thing
that is love

HEARTFULL-LESS

I loved so much that
I let my grief engulf my heart
instead of letting my heart
engulf my grief

I have so much sorrow that
I have scorched my heart and
deprived myself from compassion

BUSY SURVIVING

I'm desperate
for something
the effortless flow
that forces me to move

but I'm so tired all I
can do is sit and rest
it feels like I'm the only one
stuck buried deep under
snow as everyone else's life
waves by in sunny
days and weeks before I'm energized
enough to move again
and still
when I do move
my legs are logs
and my arms are oars
dragging through the daily
tasks of life
with my shadow growing
heavier by the hour

so I sit a lot
without energy to move
nestled in my favorite spot
on the couch
don't be mistaken thinking
I do nothing all day

for I am busy
mending the haywired
circuits in my brain
and detangling my feet to
learn these new grounds

I am busy surviving

UNFERTILE GROUNDS

I exiled myself from my community
I exiled myself from my family
I exiled myself from my heart
leaving my body in unfertile
   grounds for my soul

I put myself in this place
without really knowing
that I'd end up here

I want out of this desert

that's fine
I'll get my own self out

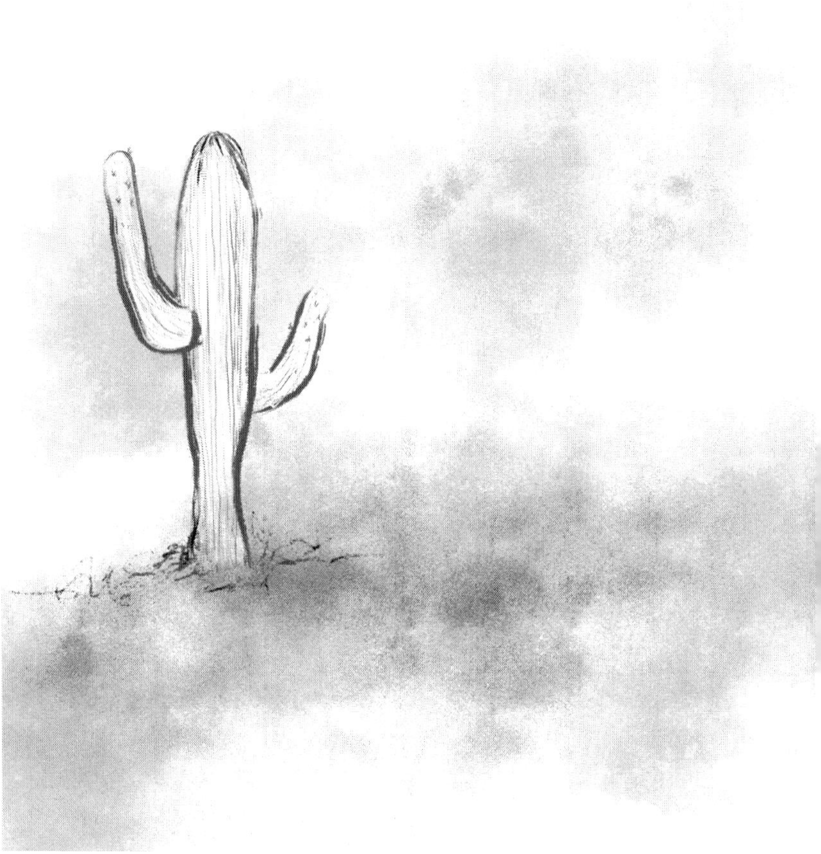

THE HEALING

PLOWING

in this country that keeps plowing forward
I had to shred away layers of
self-love in order to keep up

THE DESERT

every time I felt hurt
I banished it away

it went
down into the deeps
of me and
became so heavy
it quicksanded me
into another place
the keeper of
my soul

I want out
but don't know how
and prickly thorns
keep raging out
every time another
heart comes near

HOLD

it was too unbearable
for me to hold
and there was no one
to hold me

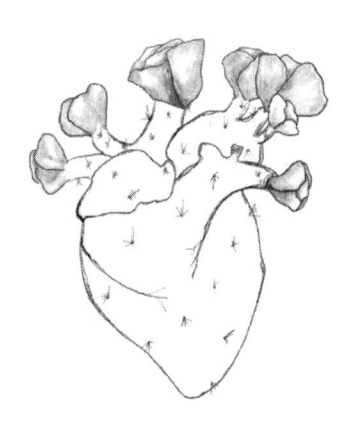

HOARDING

I wanted to preserve what
I had left of my dad
what I had left of me
little did I know
it also meant
sacrificing my living

FOOLING

if you lost a leg would you keep walking
as if nothing happened
why would you keep living
like nothing happened
when a part of your
heart died

SOUL MINE

I don't understand myself
out there
I don't understand myself
in here

so I keep looking
soul-mining for myself

KEY

you have the key
the lock is down
into the trenches
do you dare dive
deep into your wounds
to free yourself?

THE DARKNESS TO LIGHT

darkness is a resting seed
it is a gentle unfolding
of change within the cocoon of our skin
it is from this darkness that something magical is birthed
even after the darkness of dying

PERMISSION

by giving my heart permission
self-love is my shovel back to life
I am worthy of being freed

THE FORCE

I'm surrendering into
the darkness of myself
claiming stars by the hand
starting with the sun
to free all the radiance within me

I exist in the universe
and it exists in me

FINDING COMMUNITY

in my aloneness I noticed

that I have been treating
my liver separate from
my stomach
my throat separate from
my voice
my heart separate from
my mind
my body separate from
my soul

pieces of me are separated
trying to fit into
communities outside of me
stretching me even further away
from my Self
and
pieces of me trying to receive an entire
community

I now understand why it wasn't working

DECEIT

I looked back
to see
in my pictures
what my grief
looked like

all I saw
were pictures of
my kids and me
s m i l i n g

photos of events
places we visited
a distraction
that kept my
mind off of it

who was I trying to deceive?
I've certainly fooled my outer self

OLD SELF

I sat with my grief
figuring out how to live without you
and found that I am grieving my old self
learning how to live
without the person I was
when you were alive

LETTING GO

take these pathogens
I've been harboring
    in attempt to keep you alive
take the grief
I've been living
    as the only connection
I have left of you

I'm done laying here dead
you died
not me

bodies die
spirits do not

SEPARATING

I will pluck my dead self up
so that a new flower can bloom
from the sacred grounds
that hold my seeds

I am done
mourning my old self

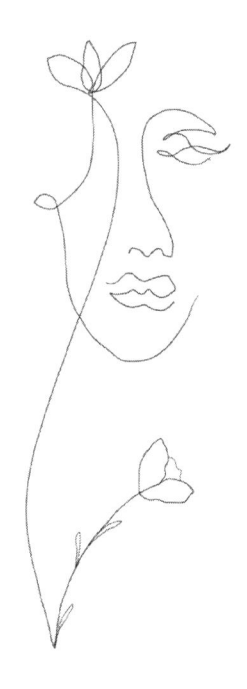

REALIZATION

if you were still alive
I'd still be hanging onto
your words your ideas and your goals for me
like a clothespin on the line

I am happy to finally let some of those things
fall away

ALTERED STATE

I wanted someone to give me a life preserver
so I could keep from sinking

I wanted someone to give me a safe house
so I could catch my bearings

I wanted someone to give me a compass
so I knew where to go

but no one gave me
any of those things

I drowned inside myself and
I found a lifeboat in my soul

a compass in my mind and heart
that showed me how to
anchor in my love

I did not have to exile myself
in order to emerge as a warrior

A RIVER OF GRIEF

my tears of raging rapids
kept at bay for so long
still not even a single drop will come out

I may not be able to cry a river of tears
but I can write a river of words
paint a canvas that speaks
until my soul is ready to release

HARD TRUST

what if I could find forgiveness
in trusting
that I did everything
I could

trust that
    for someone to be gone for good
that the reason
    must hold some truth

THE CHOICE I MADE

today, I forgive myself
for not landing softly
into the bitterness of time
for not surrendering to
your frail hands longer

BLOOMING

there is finally some light
faint but it's there
in my chest

allow me
some time to kindle it
I'm trying to keep it from flaming out

BALANCED SPACE

leave me notes in my mailbox
I'll eagerly retrieve them

come knocking on my door
I'll kick you straight to the curb

DETOUR

sometimes we take the winding detour
before we finally
come full circle
to that fork in the road
to ~~recovery~~
to ~~dealing with it~~
to making progress

ANCHORING

it occurred to me
that finding the best place to dock
is not a matter of being able to
make it through
a well-established place or
somewhere small enough
where things can be
easy and new
but a place within
on the other side
of my deepest well
where I can anchor
and push back through
me and come out anew
no matter how small or grand
the grounds I step on

CONSTELLATIONS

I'm releasing my energies like stars
where stale dreams clouding
my soul are swallowed
by black holes

where the values I hold
are diamonds that
birth constellations -
my new beautiful self

THAWING

I soften my heart
with vulnerability
so that it can
return back home to me

LITTLE REMEMBERINGS

the slurping from your afternoon tea
the rhythmic running of your
    fingertips like hoofbeats
    on the dining table

the habit of doodling in your notebooks
your jolly humming to old Hindi songs
your ALL CAP LETTERS
your games of solitaire

the meticulous combing
    of your hair and checking if
    you have everything before
    walking out the door
    wearing your brown jacket

the startle from your thunderous sneezes
the way you laughed at your own jokes

the daily things you did
I think about often
just now with less pain
and more often with a smile

INDIAN DAUGHTER

for many years
I was silently angry at you
and then forgave you
that's how I have loved you

by not being me, by being you
to call myself
your Indian daughter
my only hope
to make you proud

from a place beyond this earth
are you proud of me now?

UNCONDITIONALLY

the love and hugs
complete my heart
in dreams
when you come back for me

THE BOOK OF FORGIVENESS

I find myself rereading
all of my life's story as your daughter

pages spread out at any hour
bouncing between books of
stories with lessons
stories unfinished
stories I regret
stories that I
now see with
new eyes

I wish
there were
more stories
with happiness
yet I wallow in
the hard truth of
stories that seesaw
between fierce anger
and the raw kindness
embedded in underlying love

the cost of not belonging to myself-
conforming to your expectations
a common thread along my spine
my happiness in your hands
leaving imprints of resentment

but I am not permanently bound
to these angry thoughts
replaying in my mind
I can burn them to join your ashes
and still honor you with compassion
because even in your bitter love
my heart had a home

HOSPICE

so sure they sounded
it's time they said

I looked over to see dad's face
hoping it would match my speculation
that we need more convincing
that maybe it's too soon
to start at-home hospice
but his eyes shut and head drooped
he slept through the entire meeting
and I glanced wide-eyed back to give the nurse
an uncertain okay

just to make him more comfortable
I kept remembering
as the oxygen mask wheelchair
toilet and shower seat
came rolling in over
the next two days
we may need it in a
month or two

framed pictures decorating the dresser
got buried with stacks of
medicine and gauze
all the supplies to change his dressing
and make him more comfortable

family and close friends came
they played cards and talked
to him as he sat and nodded
listened and occasionally smiled

it was nice
but then the questions came
who were those people
after they'd leave
what day is it
after he would jerk awake

the hospital bed came rolling in
within weeks of the start of care

just to make him more comfortable

now my mom lies in the king size
while her husband lies on a folding
bed at her feet
the bedroom becoming a hospital room

the state he's in
disgraces everything he has achieved
everything he was
everything that makes him a man

I like to think he could still hear
but not aware of his lack of physicality
maybe he wouldn't have known any different
but I do
I see an intruder had kidnapped my dad
not the last memory I'd want for others

but then I understand
it wasn't for him but for the visitors
to get their closure while he's
still alive

this memory between july and august
of 2015 is hard
I should have taken that time to grieve
and be with people who loved him too
but I didn't
I shut down and plowed on
checking off lists of things to do
calling and finding a funeral home
and making sure we had all the supplies

maybe because I still couldn't face the truth
maybe I left his things on his nightstand
the way he left them
when he last touched them
because that's all that was left
of the dad I knew
the only way I want to think of dad
the part of dad that
makes me think he's still here
and thriving

ACCEPTANCE

my dad is dead
and he is not ever coming back
so of course I'm still grieving
and that's okay

DECLUTTER

it's time to
sort
discard
recycle
shred
save until I no longer need it
or choose to keep forever

it's time to declutter
my head

IDENTITY

I used to take pride
in my loneliness
distance was safer than
knowing the loss of love
it was the way my
father and his fa-
ther prayed

it was how I traveled
in all places
time gives me
but nowhere near knowing
the name of home

I am lucky to
still be
above ground
even as   a shadow

sometimes only clouds
can show you the way
to the sun

I was never meant to mute my fire
it is the element that defines me

resentment and shame linger in
the space loneliness creates

but dusts can be left behind

I gather up the precious pieces of me
all 1,825 days of it
mull them over like liquid gold

I am proud of my
scar tinted refined glass of values
my identity
the chandelier of my heart

hung up by none other
than my own two hands

losing you had me shattered
but now I shine a new light

FINDING MY OWN

we have found what
    we've been searching for
my organs
my feelings
my spirit
found each other
all within the community of my body

and now I know where I fit
in the community
around me

THE COMPASS

the best travel companion is
the working compass of the mind and the heart
having them hand in hand
makes you lost in confidence

THE LINGERING OF GRIEF

when I say grief never really goes away
don't mistake me for always being sad
I mean tomorrow will always be
another day without-
an empty hand pressed against
treasures held in the other
I mean I am always searching for the sun, for more
meanings to life
and when there is light
there is shadow
so, grief is always there

ROOM FOR JOY

just because I'm now able to feel
joy
doesn't mean I no longer feel
grief

I feel them both
they co-exist

OBLIGATIONS

how does anyone do
    all of these things
take care of their own life plus
all the inherited obligations

things to tend to
things to care for
seems to only get bigger
day by day
the caring for a parent
that many people do
but how
how do they keep sane
or do they?

how can my heart be big enough
how can my head absorb so much
to fit all of you without losing all of me

all of you that I want to absorb
and treasure before a shadow is
cast on our time but
obligations
keep getting in the way

CLEAR INTENTIONS

say yes and say no
be productive and be lazy
have the serious conversations
and have fun

it's the only way

QUARANTINE

quarantine was like our year-long personal winter

we hid from prying eyes
sat in our griefs
and met all the tiny betrayals
launching the snowball effect

it forced us to do this
to hibernate
then melt slowly
but a lockdown is not mandatory to grieve

CONSISTENTLY HEALING

I will keep seeping into the hot tub
'til the water becomes bitter
from my wounds

I will keep finding ways to release
so that I can make room for
happiness too

MOVING THROUGH

I accept the
moon waves
with open arms
because I have
the sun inside me

LIFELINE

I clung onto you as a lifeline of my existence
now I carry my name as the only reason

MEMORY IN THE WIND

but not everything has to die
you can still be
a song in the wind
a long exhale of memory

LIGHTHOUSE

I came out from the other side through
a light that could not have been found
had it not been so fearfully dark inside

FRESH PAINT

these blobs upon blobs of paint bled
until dried and cured into concrete
on the palette of my bones

these colors of
crimson and burnt umber
I now chisel and scrape away
so that the hand of my mind can wash
the bristles of my heart and dip into
the paint of infinite colors from my soul
to bring life back into my bones

THE INHERITANCE OF GRIEF

sorrows stabbing at our hearts
sufferings etched onto our souls
loss weighted in our bones
our own grief, that of our ancestors and the world

grief that always finds us
grief that is our inheritance for living

emotions rioting under our skin
sea-sand carried on our backs
disconnection jammed in our throats
from the lack of courage to ask for compassion

grief brewing in stagnant waters of shame
grief denied of its passage to feel fully

we are afraid of the truth of grief
afraid the magnitude will swallow us whole
dying and never able to fill the hole

but claim your breath
as you dive into the many little deaths
because riding through the
inheritance of your grief
gives you back your birthright to life

All THINGS IN MY REALM

I say I have been swallowed by grief
like a whole world lives inside me

I never stopped to think that
if there is darkness
there must also be light
if I'm drowning in the sea
there must also be air to breathe

I never stopped to think that
I was looking for the sun out there
when it was in here all along

LIFE

I chose life
I chose life
I chose life
I chose life
I chose life
I chose life
I chose life
I chose life
I chose life
I chose life

I'll ride the grief
journey to my soul
because
I chose L I F E

BIRTHRIGHT

as much as it is our birthright
to live and die

it is our birthright
to experience
grief and joy

WRITING

these black letters are carrying
an explosion of my emotions
in the spaces of these pages

READING

take in what you may
without obligation to respond
or the need to run away

this space is yours too

if you have so much inside of you
and have nowhere to spill it out
or just not able to find
someone to sit with
I hope that you find
a companion in these pages
to hold you and sit with you

I hope you find a thread
within these words
to carry you through moonless nights
I want you to know that you are not alone
but also that your grief is like none other

I hope you find assurance that your grief
is as real as the flesh you wear
it can change as daily as clothes
trust your wardrobe
even if it is emptiness
that hugs you
as you navigate the ebb and flow

and as abundantly devastating the loss
is burning in your heart
and smothering your soul
I hope you find compassion
for yourself - pressing
into the palette of your grief

until you find a softness
that invites curiosity

a courage to reach a little more
to rise again and again
to your new chandelier of life

ACKNOWLEDGMENTS

To my beta readers, I am overwhelmed with gratitude for your time to read this book and for your insightful feedback. Thank you, especially for your love and encouragement. You all have given me the endurance to see this book to the finish line.

To Monica and the Strive Hive family, I am indebted to every each one of you. Thank you for cheering me on and for the kick in the pants to *do-something*; for helping me water the seeds of this book. I am lucky to have such amazing friends in this community.

To William, it is such an honor to work with you. Thank you for your patience through my rewrites. It is with this wonderful balance of your thoroughness, brainstorming, and supportive comments, that has helped me become a better writer.

Warmest thank you to Veena, for being a true friend, and for being by my side through the toughest times. I cannot wait to celebrate this book with you!

To Deena, who has given me the inspiration to publish, thank you for showing me the ropes early on in my writing.

To Samir, Komal, and all of my family and friends, thank you for your continuous love and support that brings more light into my life. Special thanks to Shameem, for walking this path with my words to get to know more about Dad.

To my love Vipul, thank you for giving me confidence and unwavering support in writing this book.

To my girls, Zia and Ezri, even though you are not allowed to read this book right now, I love how supportive and proud you are that mommy is writing a poetry book. Thank you, sweeties!

To Mom, thank you for modeling how to persevere.

To Dad, thank you for loving me. Thank you for staying with me. I now release your spirits from my ribcage.

Nishi Patel is a first generation South Asian American raised by traditional Indian parents who migrated to the United States in the early 1970's.

She resides in Texas with her husband and two daughters, and has plans for more books in the future. When she is not writing or painting, Nishi enjoys time outdoors hiking and running, making memories with her family, and drinking a cup of coffee.

The Inheritance of Grief is her first poetry book.

You can find her on Instagram and TikTok
@by.nishi.patel
and on her website: www.bynishipatel.com

Made in the USA
Middletown, DE
03 September 2022